THE ROAD TO
CHRISTMAS DAY

Jan Godfrey and Marcin Piwowarski

Along the road, along the road, two thousand years ago...

Mary had a surprise visitor—a beautiful angel!

'Peace be with you,' said the angel. 'God has blessed you. You are going to have a son, a baby son, God's own Son. His name will be Jesus and you are to be his mother.'

Mary was afraid, very, very afraid, but she wanted to do as God told her.

'How can this be?' she wondered.

'God can do anything; nothing is impossible for God,'
said the angel.

    Mary looked and listened, she listened and she looked.
Then the beautiful angel went away.

Along the road, to share the news, two thousand years ago... Mary hurried to a town in the hills, to her cousin Elizabeth.

'I'm *so* happy!' said Mary. 'God has done something wonderful! He has made me the mother of a son, a baby son, God's own Son!'

Elizabeth looked and listened, she listened and she looked. Then with Mary she praised God at the wonderful news.

Along the road, along the road,
the road to Christmas Day...

Mary travelled to the little town of Bethlehem with good,
kind Joseph at her side.

'We have to be counted,' said Joseph. 'We have to go to
Bethlehem.'

Mary looked and listened, she listened and she looked.

She saw the twinkling stars along the rocky roads,
winding between the trees and houses.

She heard the donkey's hooves clip-clopping
all the way to Bethlehem.

Along the road, along the
road, the road to Christmas Day...
Mary knew that soon her
baby son would be born.

10

Mary looked and listened, she listened and she looked. She saw many people. She saw many people and donkeys. She saw many people and donkeys and luggage. She saw many people and donkeys and luggage and she heard many voices, all the way to Bethlehem.

Along the road, towards an inn, the road to Christmas Day...

Mary and Joseph knocked at doors, hoping for somewhere to stay.

Mary looked and listened, she listened and she looked. But every inn was full. Every room was taken.

Knock! 'No room!'

Knock! Knock! 'No room, no room!'

Then Joseph knocked at one more door...
'There aren't any rooms, but you can rest
out there with the animals, here
in Bethlehem.'

13

In Bethlehem, that holy night, Mary's son was born.

Mary looked and listened, she listened and she looked. She saw the ox and donkey, she saw the starry skies. She held her baby, Jesus, and heard his little cries. She wrapped him up to keep him warm, and laid him in a manger.

The Son of God was
born on earth, the very
first Christmas Day.

15

Along the road, towards the hills, the hills on Christmas Day...
Shepherds huddling with their sheep saw a bright and
glorious light!

They looked and listened, they listened and they looked.
They saw an angel, they heard good news!

'Don't be afraid,' said the angel. 'God's Son, Jesus
Christ, is born. He is born in Bethlehem today!'

The shepherds saw more angels filling the sky. They saw a dazzling, heavenly light. They saw a great host of angels and they heard songs of praise to God.

Along the road, a stony road,
the road on Christmas Day...

'Glory to God,' sang the angels. 'Peace to
all the earth.'

The shepherds looked and listened, they
listened and they looked. They saw their sheep
out on the hills, they saw the starry skies.
They hurried down to Bethlehem where
Jesus was born that night.

18

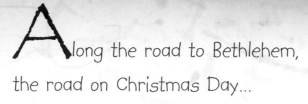

Along the road to Bethlehem,
the road on Christmas Day...
  The shepherds reached the stable and
found the baby in a manger.
  They looked and listened, they listened
and they looked.

They saw the baby sleeping in the bed Mary made for him.

They heard the animals in the stable next to the crowded inn.

'This is what the angels told us,' said the shepherds in amazement.

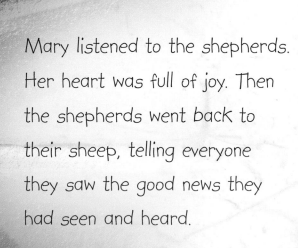

Mary listened to the shepherds. Her heart was full of joy. Then the shepherds went back to their sheep, telling everyone they saw the good news they had seen and heard.

Along the road, along the road and far away...
Wise men looked and listened, they listened and
they looked.
   They saw a new star in the sky.
They saw their camels waiting.

'A baby King has been
born!' they said. 'We must
go and find him.'

22

'We must worship him,' they said. 'We must take gifts to the baby King.'

They set off with gifts, following the star, on the long, long journey, along the road, along the road to Bethlehem.

Along the road, a long, long road, the road to find the King...
The wise men followed the star shining in the eastern sky.

24

They looked and listened, they listened
and they looked.
  'The star has come to rest!'
  'It's right over that house!'
  'It's right over that house in
Bethlehem!'

Along the road, with gifts of love, along the road to worship him...

The wise men left their camels and went into the little house.

They looked and listened, they listened and they looked.

They saw little Jesus. They saw his mother Mary.

They knelt down and worshipped him with their gifts:
gold, sweet-smelling frankincense and myrrh, fit for a King;
a heavenly, human baby King.

Along the road, the wise men rode,
along the road and home again...
    'We've seen the King, the Son of God.'
    'We've knelt and offered gifts to him.'
'We've worshipped Jesus,' the wise men said.
'We've worshipped Christ the King.'

They had looked and listened, they'd
listened and they'd looked. They had seen
the star and followed. They'd seen Jesus
and were full of joy. They'd worshipped
Christ, the baby King. Now the world was
different. It had Jesus and the very first
Christmas Day.

The Bible Reading Fellowship
15 The Chambers, Vineyard
Abingdon, OX14 3FE
United Kingdom
Tel: +44 (0)1865 319700
Email: enquiries@brf.org.uk
Website: www.brf.org.uk
ISBN 9781841016092

First edition 2008

Editorial Director Annette Reynolds
Editor Nicola Bull
Art Director Gerald Rogers
Pre-production Krystyna Kowalska Hewitt
Production John Laister

Printed and bound in Singapore